EMMANUEL JOSEPH

The Unwritten Blueprint, How
Billionaires Bend Industries to Their Will
and Redefine the Future

Copyright © 2025 by Emmanuel Joseph

All rights reserved. No part of this publication may be reproduced, stored or transmitted in any form or by any means, electronic, mechanical, photocopying, recording, scanning, or otherwise without written permission from the publisher. It is illegal to copy this book, post it to a website, or distribute it by any other means without permission.

First edition

This book was professionally typeset on Reedsy.
Find out more at reedsy.com

# Contents

1 Chapter 1: The Genesis of Billionaire Ambitions   1
2 Chapter 2: The Power of Visionary Leadership   3
3 Chapter 3: The Art of Strategic Thinking   5
4 Chapter 4: Innovation as a Driving Force   7
5 Chapter 5: Building and Sustaining a Competitive Advantage   9
6 Chapter 6: The Role of Risk-Taking in Achieving Success   11
7 Chapter 7: The Influence of Networking and Relationships   13
8 Chapter 8: The Importance of Adaptability and Resilience   15
9 Chapter 9: Leveraging Technology for Disruption   17
10 Chapter 10: The Impact of Philanthropy and Social...   19
11 Chapter 11: The Role of Mentorship and Learning   21
12 Chapter 12: The Art of Negotiation and Persuasion   23
13 Chapter 13: The Power of Branding and Marketing   25
14 Chapter 14: The Dynamics of Scaling and Expansion   27
15 Chapter 15: The Role of Culture and Values   29
16 Chapter 16: The Dynamics of Global Expansion   31
17 Chapter 17: The Legacy of Billionaires   33

# 1

# Chapter 1: The Genesis of Billionaire Ambitions

Billionaires often possess an insatiable drive that propels them toward unprecedented success. This chapter delves into the early lives of prominent billionaires, exploring how their formative years and initial experiences shaped their ambitions. From humble beginnings to privileged upbringings, the common thread is their relentless pursuit of excellence. Whether it was a spark of inspiration, an influential mentor, or a pivotal moment, these individuals harnessed their unique experiences to set ambitious goals and navigate the complexities of the business world.

Their journeys are marked by a combination of innate talent, strategic thinking, and sheer determination. They identified opportunities where others saw obstacles and dared to take calculated risks. These early chapters of their lives are filled with stories of perseverance, failures, and hard-won successes that laid the foundation for their future empires. As they honed their skills and expanded their networks, they began to see the world through a lens of infinite possibilities.

The desire to innovate and disrupt established industries became a driving force for these visionaries. They were not content with the status quo and constantly sought ways to challenge conventional wisdom. Through a series of bold decisions and groundbreaking ideas, they started to carve out niches in various industries. This chapter highlights the importance of nurturing one's ambitions and the transformative power of dreaming big.

Ultimately, the genesis of billionaire ambitions is a testament to the human spirit's resilience and creativity. By understanding the origins of their drive, we gain insights into the qualities that set these individuals apart and inspire us to pursue our own dreams with unwavering determination.

# 2

# Chapter 2: The Power of Visionary Leadership

Visionary leadership is a hallmark of billionaires who have reshaped industries and redefined the future. This chapter explores the qualities and strategies that make these leaders stand out. At the core of their success is the ability to articulate a compelling vision that inspires and mobilizes others. They possess a unique combination of foresight, charisma, and the ability to translate abstract ideas into tangible goals.

Visionary leaders are adept at identifying emerging trends and anticipating market shifts. They have a keen sense of timing and are not afraid to invest in disruptive technologies and innovative business models. By fostering a culture of creativity and collaboration, they empower their teams to think outside the box and push the boundaries of what's possible. This chapter delves into the stories of iconic leaders who have successfully navigated the complexities of their industries and left an indelible mark on the world.

In addition to their strategic acumen, visionary leaders are also exceptional communicators. They know how to convey their vision in a way that resonates with stakeholders, from employees to investors. Their ability to inspire confidence and align diverse interests is crucial in rallying support for ambitious projects. This chapter examines the communication strategies and storytelling techniques that have enabled these leaders to build loyal followings and drive transformative change.

Ultimately, visionary leadership is about more than just setting a direction; it's about creating a shared sense of purpose and fostering a culture of innovation. By understanding the principles of visionary leadership, we can learn how to harness our own potential and lead with impact.

# 3

# Chapter 3: The Art of Strategic Thinking

Strategic thinking is a critical skill that distinguishes successful billionaires from their peers. This chapter explores the art of crafting and executing strategies that drive long-term success. At its core, strategic thinking involves the ability to analyze complex situations, identify key drivers of change, and make informed decisions that align with overarching goals.

Billionaires are masters of strategic thinking, able to anticipate market trends and adapt to evolving conditions. They approach problems with a holistic perspective, considering both short-term gains and long-term implications. By leveraging data and insights, they develop strategies that are both innovative and grounded in reality. This chapter delves into the thought processes and frameworks used by billionaires to navigate uncertainty and seize opportunities.

A key aspect of strategic thinking is the ability to remain flexible and agile. Billionaires understand that the business landscape is constantly evolving, and they are prepared to pivot when necessary. This chapter examines the importance of adaptability and resilience in the face of challenges. By embracing change and staying open to new ideas, these leaders are able to stay ahead of the curve and maintain their competitive edge.

In addition to their analytical skills, billionaires also possess a strong intuition that guides their decision-making. They have a knack for spotting trends and recognizing patterns that others might overlook. This chapter explores how they balance data-driven analysis with gut instincts to make strategic choices that propel their businesses forward. Ultimately, the art of strategic thinking is about combining foresight, creativity, and discipline to achieve extraordinary results.

# 4

# Chapter 4: Innovation as a Driving Force

Innovation is the lifeblood of industries and a key factor in the success of billionaires. This chapter delves into the role of innovation in transforming industries and redefining the future. Billionaires are often at the forefront of technological advancements and groundbreaking ideas that disrupt traditional business models. They are not afraid to challenge the status quo and experiment with novel approaches.

The ability to foster a culture of innovation is a defining characteristic of successful billionaires. They create environments where creativity is encouraged, and failure is seen as a stepping stone to success. This chapter explores the strategies and practices that billionaires use to cultivate innovation within their organizations. From investing in research and development to fostering collaboration and cross-functional teams, they create ecosystems that thrive on new ideas and continuous improvement.

Innovation is also about recognizing opportunities where others see obstacles. Billionaires have a unique ability to identify unmet needs and develop solutions that address them. This chapter highlights the stories of entrepreneurs who have revolutionized industries through innovative products and services. By staying ahead of the curve and anticipating market demands, they are able to create value and drive growth.

Ultimately, innovation is a mindset that requires a willingness to take risks and embrace change. This chapter examines the qualities and behaviors that enable billionaires to think creatively and push the boundaries of what's possible. By understanding the principles of innovation, we can learn how to harness our own creativity and drive positive change in our own lives and industries.

# 5

# Chapter 5: Building and Sustaining a Competitive Advantage

Creating a sustainable competitive advantage is a key factor in the long-term success of billionaires. This chapter explores the strategies and practices that billionaires use to build and maintain their competitive edge. At the heart of their success is the ability to differentiate themselves from their competitors and deliver unique value to their customers.

Billionaires understand the importance of developing a deep understanding of their target market and identifying key differentiators. They invest in market research and customer insights to create products and services that meet the needs and preferences of their audience. This chapter delves into the tactics and techniques that billionaires use to create a strong brand identity and build customer loyalty.

In addition to product differentiation, billionaires also focus on operational excellence. They are constantly looking for ways to improve efficiency and reduce costs. This chapter examines the role of technology and innovation in streamlining operations and enhancing productivity. By leveraging data and automation, they are able to optimize their processes and deliver superior value to their customers.

Ultimately, building and sustaining a competitive advantage requires a combination of strategic thinking, innovation, and execution. This chapter explores the principles and practices that enable billionaires to stay ahead of the competition and drive long-term success. By understanding the factors that contribute to a competitive advantage, we can learn how to create value and achieve our own goals.

# 6

# Chapter 6: The Role of Risk-Taking in Achieving Success

R isk-taking is an essential component of success for billionaires. This chapter explores the role of calculated risks in achieving extraordinary results. Billionaires are known for their willingness to take bold risks and make decisions that others might shy away from. They understand that with great risk comes the potential for great reward.

At the core of their risk-taking mindset is a thorough understanding of the potential outcomes and a willingness to embrace uncertainty. Billionaires conduct extensive research and analysis to assess the risks and benefits of their decisions. This chapter delves into the strategies and frameworks that billionaires use to evaluate and manage risks.

In addition to their analytical skills, billionaires also possess a strong sense of intuition and confidence in their abilities. They trust their instincts and are not afraid to take decisive action. This chapter examines the importance of self-belief and resilience in the face of challenges. By staying focused on their goals and maintaining a positive mindset, they are able to navigate uncertainty and overcome obstacles.

Ultimately, risk-taking is about balancing caution with ambition. This chapter explores the qualities and behaviors that enable billionaires to take calculated risks and achieve extraordinary success. By understanding the principles of risk-taking, we can learn how to embrace uncertainty and pursue our own goals with confidence.

# 7

# Chapter 7: The Influence of Networking and Relationships

Networking and relationships are crucial factors in the success of billionaires. This chapter explores the role of building and maintaining strong networks in achieving extraordinary results. Billionaires understand the importance of connecting with influential individuals and leveraging their networks to gain access to valuable resources and opportunities.

At the core of their networking strategy is the ability to build genuine relationships based on trust and mutual benefit. Billionaires are skilled at identifying and cultivating relationships with key stakeholders, from mentors and advisors to investors and partners. This chapter delves into the tactics and techniques that billionaires use to build and maintain strong networks.

In addition to building relationships, billionaires also focus on creating value for their networks. They are constantly looking for ways to provide support and assistance to their connections. This chapter examines the importance of reciprocity and collaboration in building strong networks. By fostering a culture of mutual benefit, billionaires are able to create a network of supporters who are invested in their success.

Ultimately, networking and relationships are about more than just making connections; they are about creating a community of individuals who share a common vision and are committed to helping each other achieve their goals. This chapter explores the principles and practices that enable billionaires to build and maintain strong networks and achieve extraordinary success. By understanding the factors that

By understanding the factors that contribute to successful networking and relationships, we can learn how to build our own networks and leverage them to achieve our goals.

# 8

# Chapter 8: The Importance of Adaptability and Resilience

Adaptability and resilience are crucial qualities for billionaires who have achieved extraordinary success. This chapter explores the importance of staying flexible and resilient in the face of challenges and uncertainty. Billionaires understand that the business landscape is constantly evolving, and they are prepared to adapt to changing conditions.

At the core of their adaptability is the ability to embrace change and stay open to new ideas. Billionaires are not afraid to pivot and explore new opportunities when necessary. This chapter examines the importance of staying agile and responsive in a rapidly changing world. By remaining flexible and adaptable, billionaires are able to navigate uncertainty and seize opportunities.

Resilience is also a key factor in the success of billionaires. They possess a strong sense of determination and perseverance that enables them to overcome obstacles and bounce back from setbacks. This chapter delves into the strategies and practices that billionaires use to build and maintain their resilience. From developing a positive mindset to building a support network, they create a foundation of strength and resilience that enables them to thrive in the face of challenges.

Ultimately, adaptability and resilience are about more than just surviving;

they are about thriving in a constantly changing world. This chapter explores the qualities and behaviors that enable billionaires to stay flexible and resilient and achieve extraordinary success. By understanding the principles of adaptability and resilience, we can learn how to navigate uncertainty and pursue our own goals with confidence.

# 9

# Chapter 9: Leveraging Technology for Disruption

Technology is a powerful tool for disruption and transformation. This chapter explores how billionaires leverage technology to create innovative solutions and reshape industries. Billionaires are often at the forefront of technological advancements, investing in cutting-edge technologies that have the potential to revolutionize their businesses.

At the core of their success is the ability to identify and harness the potential of emerging technologies. Billionaires are constantly looking for ways to incorporate new technologies into their operations and create value for their customers. This chapter delves into the strategies and practices that billionaires use to leverage technology for disruption.

In addition to adopting new technologies, billionaires also invest in research and development to create proprietary solutions that give them a competitive edge. This chapter examines the importance of innovation and experimentation in developing technological solutions that drive growth and transformation. By fostering a culture of innovation and investing in technology, billionaires are able to stay ahead of the curve and maintain their competitive edge.

Ultimately, leveraging technology for disruption requires a combination of strategic thinking, innovation, and execution. This chapter explores the principles and practices that enable billionaires to harness the power of technology and achieve extraordinary success. By understanding the role of technology in driving disruption, we can learn how to leverage it to create value and achieve our own goals.

# 10

## Chapter 10: The Impact of Philanthropy and Social Responsibility

Philanthropy and social responsibility are important aspects of the success of billionaires. This chapter explores the role of giving back and making a positive impact on society. Billionaires understand that their success comes with a responsibility to contribute to the greater good.

At the core of their philanthropic efforts is the desire to create positive change and make a difference in the world. Billionaires invest in causes that align with their values and have the potential to create lasting impact. This chapter delves into the strategies and practices that billionaires use to drive social change and give back to their communities.

In addition to their philanthropic efforts, billionaires also focus on creating socially responsible businesses. They understand the importance of sustainability and ethical practices in building a successful and sustainable business. This chapter examines the role of corporate social responsibility in driving long-term success and creating value for all stakeholders.

Ultimately, philanthropy and social responsibility are about more than just giving back; they are about creating a legacy of positive impact. This chapter explores the qualities and behaviors that enable billionaires to drive social change and achieve extraordinary success. By understanding the principles of philanthropy and social responsibility, we can learn how to make a positive impact and contribute to the greater good.

# 11

# Chapter 11: The Role of Mentorship and Learning

Mentorship and continuous learning are crucial factors in the success of billionaires. This chapter explores the importance of seeking guidance and investing in personal and professional development. Billionaires understand that learning is a lifelong journey and that mentorship is a valuable tool for growth and development.

At the core of their success is the ability to seek out and learn from mentors and advisors. Billionaires surround themselves with individuals who have the experience and expertise to guide them on their journey. This chapter delves into the strategies and practices that billionaires use to build and maintain strong mentorship relationships.

In addition to seeking guidance from mentors, billionaires also invest in continuous learning and development. They are constantly looking for ways to expand their knowledge and skills, staying ahead of the curve in their industries. This chapter examines the importance of a growth mindset and the willingness to embrace new challenges and opportunities.

Ultimately, mentorship and learning are about more than just acquiring knowledge; they are about building a foundation of growth and development that enables billionaires to achieve extraordinary success. This chapter explores the qualities and behaviors that enable billionaires to seek out mentorship and invest in continuous learning. By understanding the principles of mentorship and learning, we can learn how to grow and develop our own potential.

# 12

# Chapter 12: The Art of Negotiation and Persuasion

Negotiation and persuasion are critical skills for billionaires who have achieved extraordinary success. This chapter explores the art of negotiating and persuading others to achieve desired outcomes. Billionaires understand the importance of effective communication and the ability to influence and persuade others.

At the core of their success is the ability to build rapport and establish trust with their counterparts. Billionaires are skilled at understanding the needs and motivations of others and crafting compelling arguments that resonate with their audience. This chapter delves into the strategies and practices that billionaires use to negotiate and persuade effectively.

In addition to building rapport and crafting compelling arguments, billionaires also focus on creating win-win solutions that benefit all parties involved. They understand that successful negotiations are about finding common ground and creating value for all stakeholders. This chapter examines the importance of collaboration and compromise in achieving successful outcomes.

Ultimately, negotiation and persuasion are about more than just achieving desired outcomes; they are about building strong relationships and creating value for all parties involved. This chapter explores the qualities and behaviors that enable billionaires to negotiate and persuade effectively and achieve extraordinary success. By understanding the principles of negotiation and persuasion, we can learn how to influence and persuade others to achieve our own goals.

# 13

# Chapter 13: The Power of Branding and Marketing

Branding and marketing are essential components of the success of billionaires. This chapter explores the role of building a strong brand and effective marketing strategies in achieving extraordinary results. Billionaires understand the importance of creating a compelling brand identity and communicating their value proposition to their target audience.

At the core of their success is the ability to understand their target market and craft messaging that resonates with their audience. Billionaires invest in market research and customer insights to create marketing strategies that are both effective and impactful. This chapter delves into the tactics and techniques that billionaires use to build and maintain strong brands.

In addition to crafting compelling messaging, billionaires also focus on creating memorable experiences for their customers. They understand that branding is about more than just a logo or a tagline; it is about creating a consistent and cohesive experience that reflects their values and vision. This chapter examines the importance of customer experience in building a strong brand and driving customer loyalty.

Ultimately, branding and marketing are about more than just promoting products and services; they are about creating a connection with customers and building a loyal following. This chapter explores the qualities and behaviors that enable billionaires to build strong brands and achieve extraordinary success. By understanding the principles of branding and marketing, we can learn how to create compelling brands and communicate our value proposition effectively.

# 14

# Chapter 14: The Dynamics of Scaling and Expansion

Scaling and expansion are critical factors in the success of billionaires who have built large and influential businesses. This chapter explores the dynamics of growing and expanding businesses to achieve extraordinary results. Billionaires understand the importance of scaling their operations and entering new markets to drive growth and create value.

At the core of their success is the ability to develop and execute strategic plans for scaling and expansion. Billionaires are skilled at identifying opportunities for growth and creating strategies to capitalize on them. This chapter delves into the tactics and techniques that billionaires use to scale their businesses and expand into new markets.

In addition to developing strategic plans, billionaires also focus on building the infrastructure and capabilities needed to support growth. They invest in technology, talent, and processes to ensure that their businesses can scale effectively. This chapter examines the importance of building a strong foundation for growth and creating a scalable business model.

Ultimately, scaling and expansion are about more than just growing a business; they are about creating sustainable and long-term success. This chapter explores the qualities and behaviors that enable billionaires to scale their businesses and achieve extraordinary success. By understanding the principles of scaling and expansion, we can learn how to grow our own businesses and achieve our goals.

# 15

# Chapter 15: The Role of Culture and Values

Culture and values are essential components of the success of billionaires and their businesses. This chapter explores the role of creating a strong organizational culture and aligning values with business strategies to achieve extraordinary results. Billionaires understand the importance of building a positive and cohesive culture that reflects their vision and values.

At the core of their success is the ability to create a culture of excellence and innovation. Billionaires foster an environment where creativity and collaboration are encouraged, and employees are empowered to take risks and experiment with new ideas. This chapter delves into the strategies and practices that billionaires use to build and maintain a strong organizational culture.

In addition to fostering a culture of excellence, billionaires also focus on aligning their values with their business strategies. They understand that a strong sense of purpose and shared values are crucial in driving employee engagement and customer loyalty. This chapter examines the importance

This chapter examines the importance of aligning values with business strategies to create a sense of purpose and direction for the entire organization. By fostering a culture that reflects their values, billionaires are able to build strong, cohesive teams and drive long-term success. This chapter explores the principles and practices that enable billionaires to create a positive organizational culture and achieve extraordinary results. By understanding the role of culture and values, we can learn how to build and maintain a strong organizational culture and align our values with our business strategies.

# 16

# Chapter 16: The Dynamics of Global Expansion

Global expansion is a critical factor in the success of billionaires who have built large and influential businesses. This chapter explores the dynamics of entering new international markets and achieving extraordinary results on a global scale. Billionaires understand the importance of expanding their operations beyond their home markets to drive growth and create value.

At the core of their success is the ability to develop and execute strategic plans for global expansion. Billionaires are skilled at identifying opportunities in new markets and creating strategies to capitalize on them. This chapter delves into the tactics and techniques that billionaires use to expand their businesses internationally and navigate the complexities of global markets.

In addition to developing strategic plans, billionaires also focus on building the infrastructure and capabilities needed to support global expansion. They invest in technology, talent, and processes to ensure that their businesses can operate effectively in diverse markets. This chapter examines the importance of building a strong foundation for global growth and creating a scalable business model.

Ultimately, global expansion is about more than just entering new markets; it is about creating sustainable and long-term success on a global scale.

This chapter explores the qualities and behaviors that enable billionaires to expand their businesses internationally and achieve extraordinary success. By understanding the principles of global expansion, we can learn how to grow our own businesses and achieve our goals on a global scale.

# 17

## Chapter 17: The Legacy of Billionaires

The legacy of billionaires is a testament to their extraordinary achievements and the impact they have had on the world. This chapter explores the lasting influence of billionaires and the lessons we can learn from their success. Billionaires understand the importance of leaving a lasting legacy that reflects their values and vision.

At the core of their legacy is the ability to create positive change and make a difference in the world. Billionaires invest in causes and initiatives that have the potential to create lasting impact and drive social change. This chapter delves into the strategies and practices that billionaires use to build their legacy and leave a positive mark on the world.

In addition to their philanthropic efforts, billionaires also focus on creating sustainable and ethical businesses that reflect their values. They understand the importance of building businesses that are not only successful but also socially responsible. This chapter examines the importance of corporate social responsibility and ethical practices in building a lasting legacy.

Ultimately, the legacy of billionaires is about more than just their financial success; it is about the positive impact they have had on the world and the lessons we can learn from their journey. This chapter explores the qualities and behaviors that enable billionaires to build their legacy and achieve extraordinary success. By understanding the principles of legacy-building, we can learn how to create a positive impact and leave our own mark on the world.

**"The Unwritten Blueprint: How Billionaires Bend Industries to Their Will and Redefine the Future**" is an insightful journey into the minds and strategies of the world's most successful billionaires. This book explores the unique qualities and approaches that set these individuals apart, allowing them to reshape entire industries and drive innovation on a global scale.

Through 17 engaging chapters, readers will discover the importance of visionary leadership, strategic thinking, and calculated risk-taking in achieving extraordinary success. The book delves into the power of adaptability, resilience, and innovation, highlighting how billionaires leverage these traits to stay ahead of the competition and create lasting impact.

Additionally, "The Unwritten Blueprint" examines the role of networking, mentorship, and continuous learning in building strong relationships and driving personal and professional growth. It also explores the importance of philanthropy and social responsibility, showcasing how billionaires give back to their communities and make a positive difference in the world.

By understanding the principles and practices that have enabled billionaires to achieve unparalleled success, readers will gain valuable insights and inspiration to pursue their own dreams and redefine their future. This book is a must-read for anyone looking to learn from the best and apply their strategies to achieve their own goals.

www.ingramcontent.com/pod-product-compliance
Lightning Source LLC
LaVergne TN
LVHW020500080526
838202LV00057B/6060